A LOVE WITHOUT END

C.B. JACKSON

Wingspan Press

Published in the United States and the United Kingdom
by WingSpan Press, Livermore, CA

The WingSpan name, logo and colophon are the trademarks of WingSpan Publishing.

Publisher's Cataloging-in-Publication data

Names: Jackson, C. B., author.
Title: A love without end / written and illustrated by C. B. Jackson.
Description: Livermore, CA: Wingspan Press, 2023. | Summary: Katrina's mother dies and a stuffed rabbit helps her through her grief.
Identifiers: LCCN: 2023915940 | ISBN: 978-1-63683-056-8 (paperback) | 978-1-63683-955-4 (ebook)
Subjects: LCSH Grief--Juvenile fiction. | Death--Juvenile fiction. | Bereavement in children--Juvenile fiction. | BISAC JUVENILE FICTION / Social Themes / Death, Grief, Bereavement
Classification: LCC PZ7.1 .J33 Lo 2023 | DDC [E]--dc23

Printed in the United States of America

www.wingspanpress.com

Dedication

Losing a parent, no matter what age you are, is such a blow to the heart. Navigating this world on our own without that sacred person to guide us, comfort us and to just be there for us, is a lonely place to be.

This book was written for those of you who are experiencing this separation. It is my one way of giving you some "comforting arms" in another way. I cannot allay your grief, but I can hold you in my heart while you weather the storm.

With loving reverence,
C.B. J.

A special thanks to Quincy and Erin. You made this possible and I love you for that.

A LOVE WITHOUT END

Katrina lay in her bed staring at the large shadows on the wall. She knew they were cast by the familiar toys she loved, but it was hard not to feel frightened.

Why did the dark feel like this? "What is this other strange feeling I'm having?" Katrina thought to herself. It felt like a stomach ache, but she knew she was not sick. She tried to ignore it, hoping it would go away. If she could just fall asleep. Soon she did.

But as Katrina slept, she began to have a bad dream. In this nightmare it was very dark and wet. She tried to run because something big and scary was chasing her. But she could not escape.

She woke up suddenly feeling very frightened. She was breathing very hard and her heart was beating very fast, as if she actually had been running. She wanted so much for someone to hold her to make her feel safe and warm. That's when it became real clear in her mind why she had been having so many aches and pains. She missed her mother.

Katrina could not hold back the flood of tears that came streaming out of her eyes. The pillow, where her face lay, became soaked with tears. She felt as if her heart was about to break from the sadness, when she just faintly heard a soft voice.

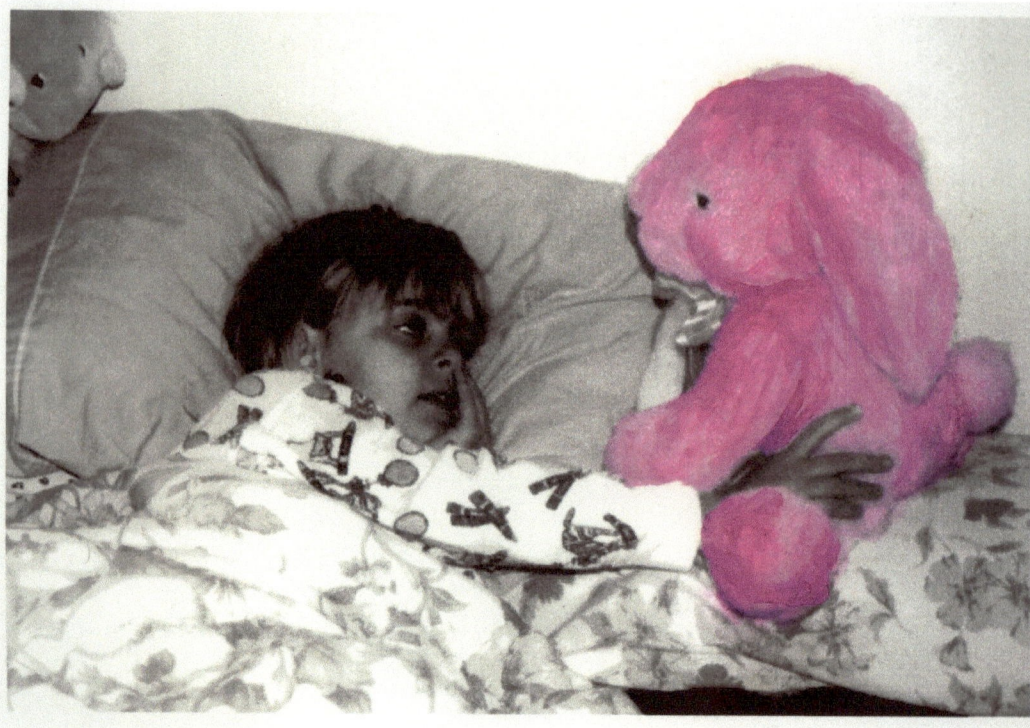

Her sobbing quieted down as she wiped her eyes and looked towards the direction of this gentle sound. She thought maybe she had imagined it, but then she heard it again. This time it was coming from the pink rabbit beside her.

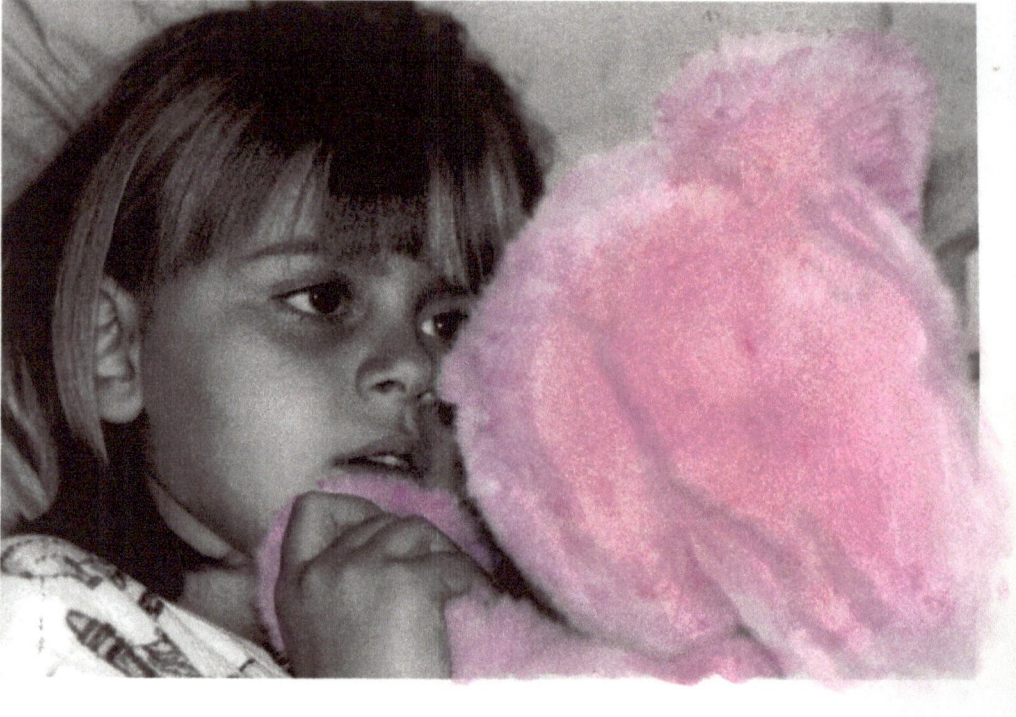

His deep eyes glowed lightly in the darkness as he reached for her with his fluffy short arms. He asked, "Why do you cry little one?" "Oh Harey", she sobbed again and fell into his loving pink arms, "I want my Mommy".

Harey comforted her and said, "Yes, I know you do. I wish you could be with her too. But can I tell you a story?" Again, Katrina wiped her face and looked at him longingly, answering, "Yes, oh yes, I would like that."

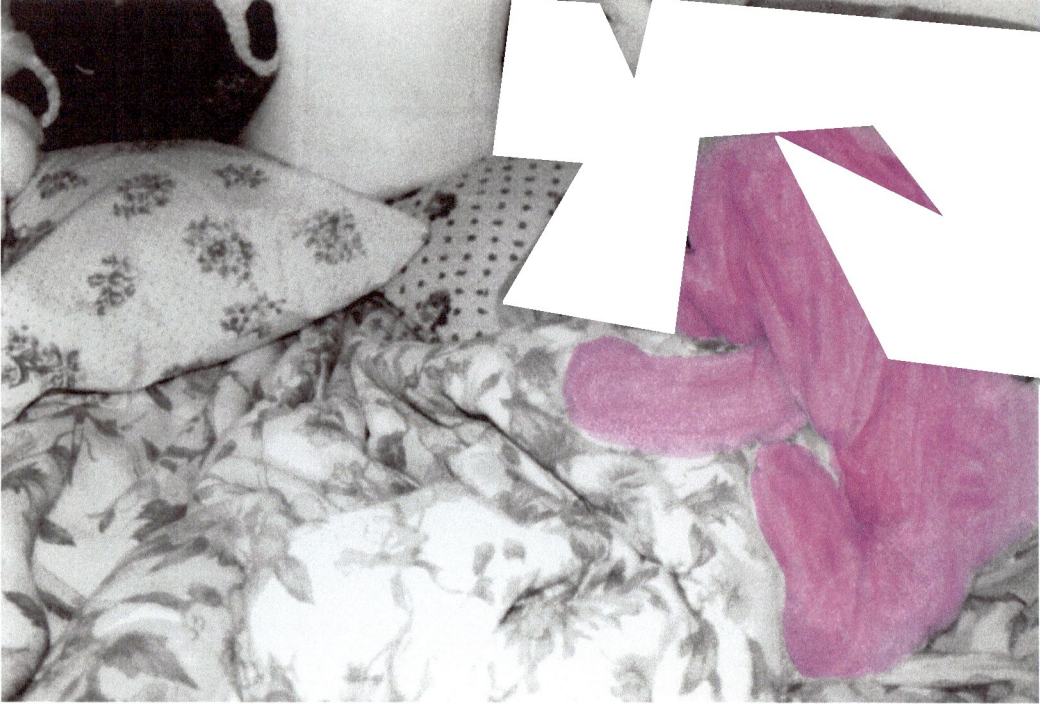

"Okay", Harey instructed, "lay your sweet head back down on the pillow and I will tell you this story." Katrina nestled herself back onto the pillow and pulled the covers up around her. She began to feel very cozy.

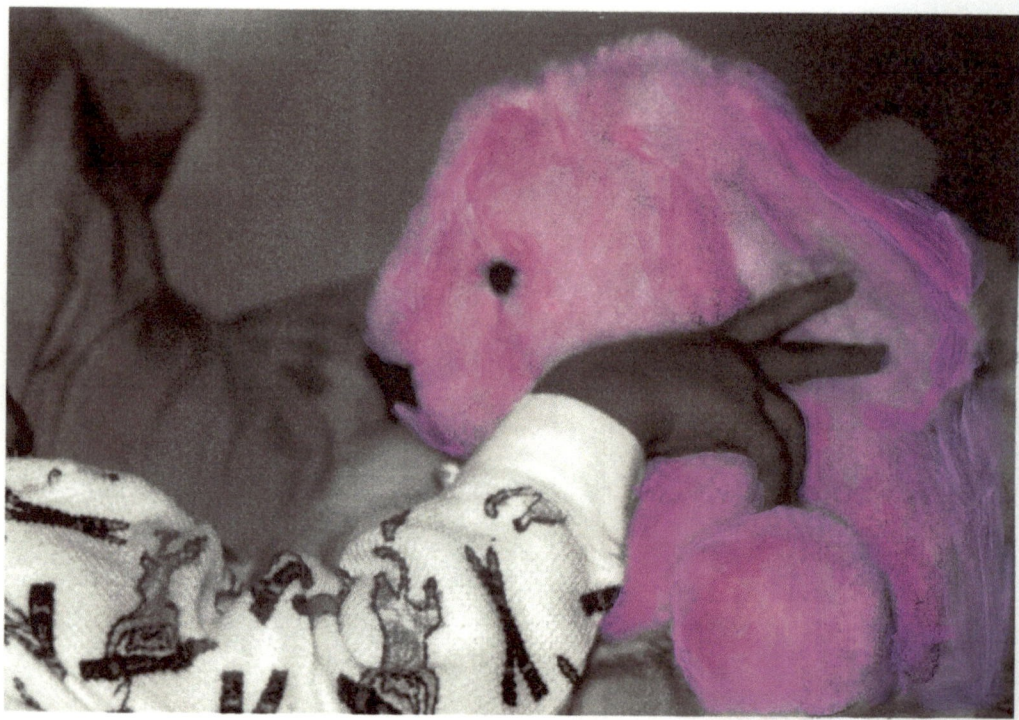

Harey began, "There once was a beautiful woman and her name was Sierra." Katrina sat straight up and blurted out, "That's my mother's name!" Harey tried his best to look surprised and replied, "It was!?" Well, that IS a coincidence. That makes this story even more special then."

Katrina lay back down feeling even more warm inside. She was relishing every word Harey had to say, as if every sentence was the sweetest treat she had ever tasted.

Harey continued, "Sierra was on a journey. A long journey. She walked along the path that led to the place she had to get to. With each step she observed all the different sights on the way. Some things were beautiful and interesting and some were not so beautiful. But, all was fascinating to her. Sometimes the path became difficult and hard to see, but she kept on going, knowing she was headed in the right direction. But the one thing on this path, the most wonderful thing that brought her so much joy, was the little girl she walked with on the way. Katy.

The journey was such a joy to Sierra while Katy was with her. They walked hand in hand together. They would stop along the way to breathe the aroma of the flowers. They would marvel at all the different things life had to offer.

Katy and Sierra loved each other so much that they hardly even noticed how hard the journey became sometimes. The time just flew by. They were together and that's all that mattered.

One day they came to a fork in the road. Only this split did not go left or right. That way they could have both taken the same direction together. This fork went up and down. Sierra turned to Katy as she kneeled down in front of her, looking into her big beautiful eyes and said, "Katy, I have to take this other path now and it's not time for you to take it too. It will seem like we are apart. I don't really want to be away from you, but it's only for a short while. Even though you can't see me with your eyes or feel me with your arms, I am still going to be near you. Can you believe that until I see you again?"

Katy felt something swell up in her throat and her chest began to hurt something fierce. But she trusted Sierra completely and forced out, "Yes I will". "Okay then", Sierra sighed as she stood up still holding both of Katy's hands, "that's my brave girl". Her voice trailed off in the air and in a blink of Katy's eyes, Sierra had turned into a radiant white bird and flew gracefully upward.

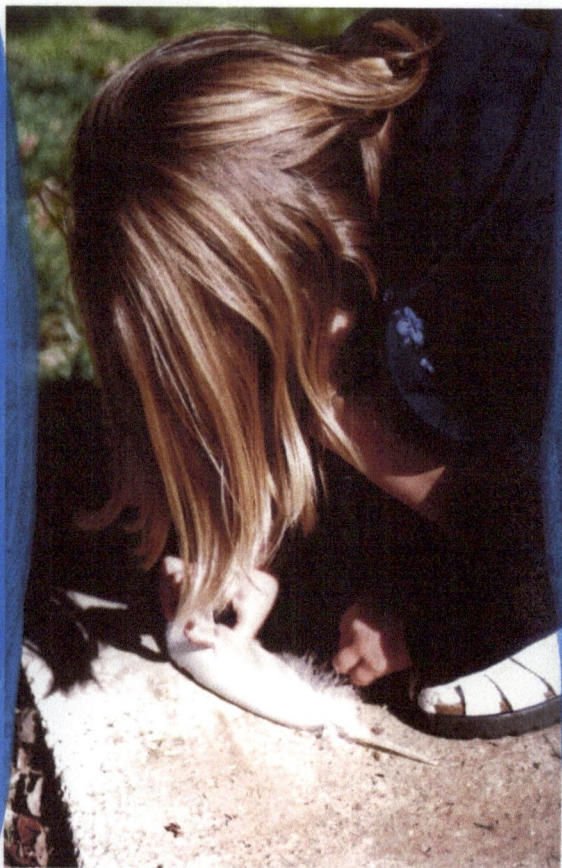

Katy stood there with tears running down her face, when she looked down on the ground only to see a large white feather laying at her feet. She picked it up and knew it was left behind by Sierra. She realized it would always remind her that Sierra was near and watching over her. Katy went on her way down the path with the feather in her hand and she could still feel Sierra's hand in her's. She began to hum a little tune that they always sang together. Although she felt alone, she knew she was not alone and that she would be alright until she could be with Sierra again.

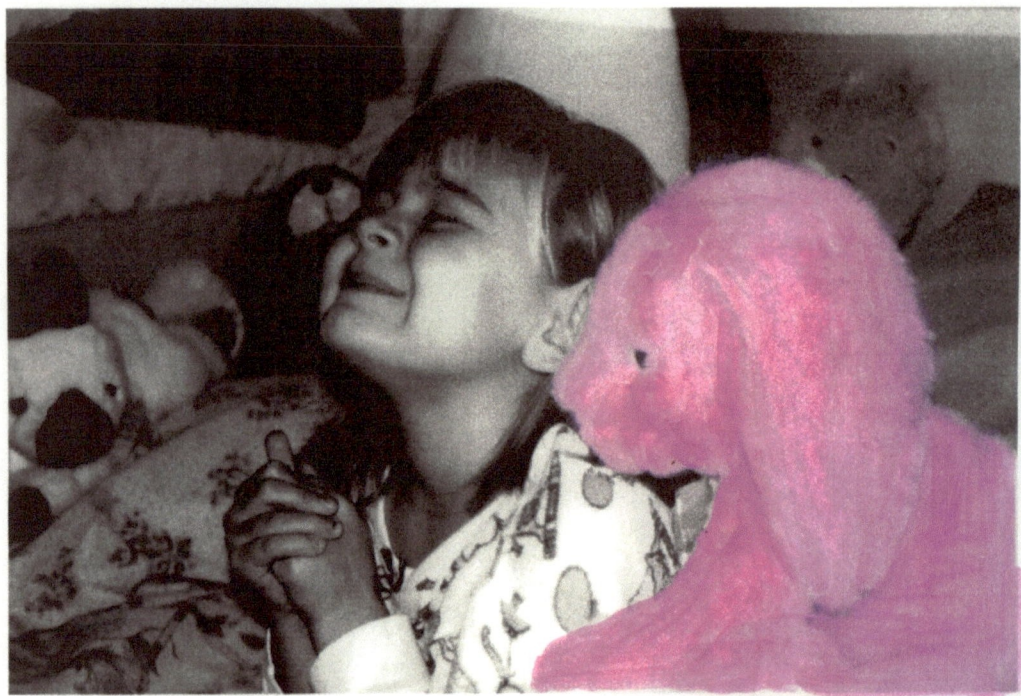

Harey stopped and looked at Katrina, who was looking at him with tears streaking her cheeks. She inquired in between sobs, "That story was about my Mom and me, wasn't it Harey?" "Yes," he admitted, "it was." "Is she really here Harey?" Katrina urged. "Yes, Katrina, she is here. I bet if you look into your heart very quietly, you will see her. Because, as long as you are alive and feel her in your heart, she is still alive too." "I'm going to close my eyes and look right now," Katrina said with anticipation. "That's good," Harey encouraged, "I'll sit right here while you do that".

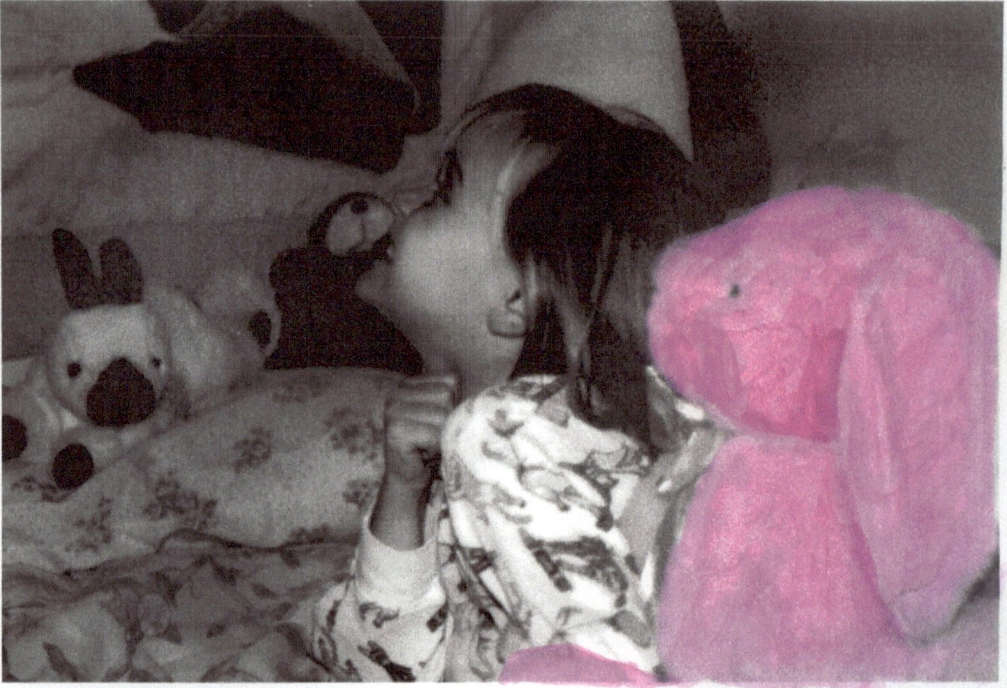

She took a deep breath and saw the pictures of her mother in her mind. Yes, she could feel her presence. She opened her eyes to share the news with Harey, when suddenly, she saw a glowing vision just above her bed.

There was a colorful cloud and on it was a beautiful angel who looked at her with so much love in her eyes. It was her mother. Katrina blurted out, "Mama!" "Yes, Baby, I am here," her mother replied. "You can see me now because you opened your heart. I will never leave you. Can you remember that?" "Oh yes Mama, I can. I will!" Katrina implored.

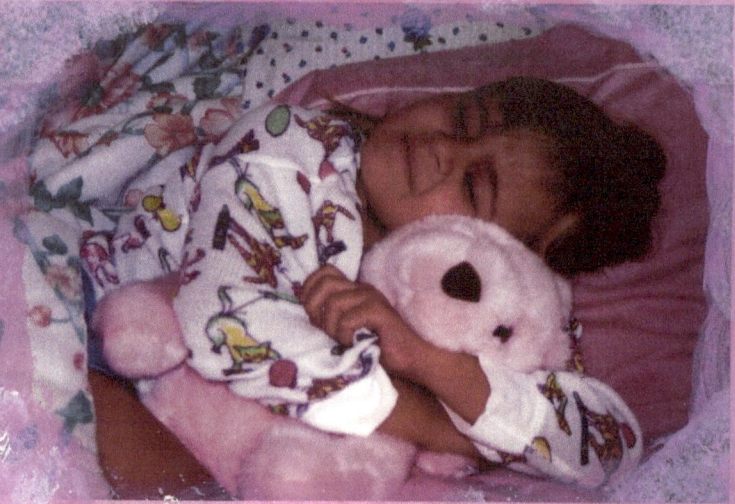

"Okay, Sweetheart," her mother whispered, "then you close your eyes and sleep now, because we can be together in your dreams too." "Alright Mama", Katrina wearily sighed. She closed her eyes and pulled Harey close to her, snuggling with him and feeling very warm and safe.

Harey spoke softly in her ear as she began to drop off to sleep, "And Katrina?" "Yes Harey", she wisped. "Just know that it's okay to cry when you're missing her. That's also the love you feel for her when you're remembering her. Just hold me close whenever you need to, because my fuzzy hands will catch all those tears and send them straight up to heaven as love notes to your Mom. Is that a deal?" "Deal, Harey", Katrina sighed as she squeezed him even tighter and fell into a deep sleep. There, she and her Mom danced in a bright field of flowers----------------singing and laughing.

.

www.ingramcontent.com/pod-product-compliance
Lightning Source LLC
Chambersburg PA
CBHW042107110426
42742CB00033BA/25